3 Gymnopédies

By

Erik Satie

For Solo Piano

(1888)

Read & Co.

Copyright © 2021 Read & Co. Books

This edition is published by Read & Co. Books,
an imprint of Read & Co.

This book is copyright and may not be reproduced or copied in any way without the express permission of the publisher in writing.

British Library Cataloguing-in-Publication Data
A catalogue record for this book is available
from the British Library.

Read & Co. is part of Read Books Ltd.
For more information visit
www.readandcobooks.co.uk

à Mademoiselle JEANNE de BRET

1ᵉʳᵉ GYMNOPÉDIE

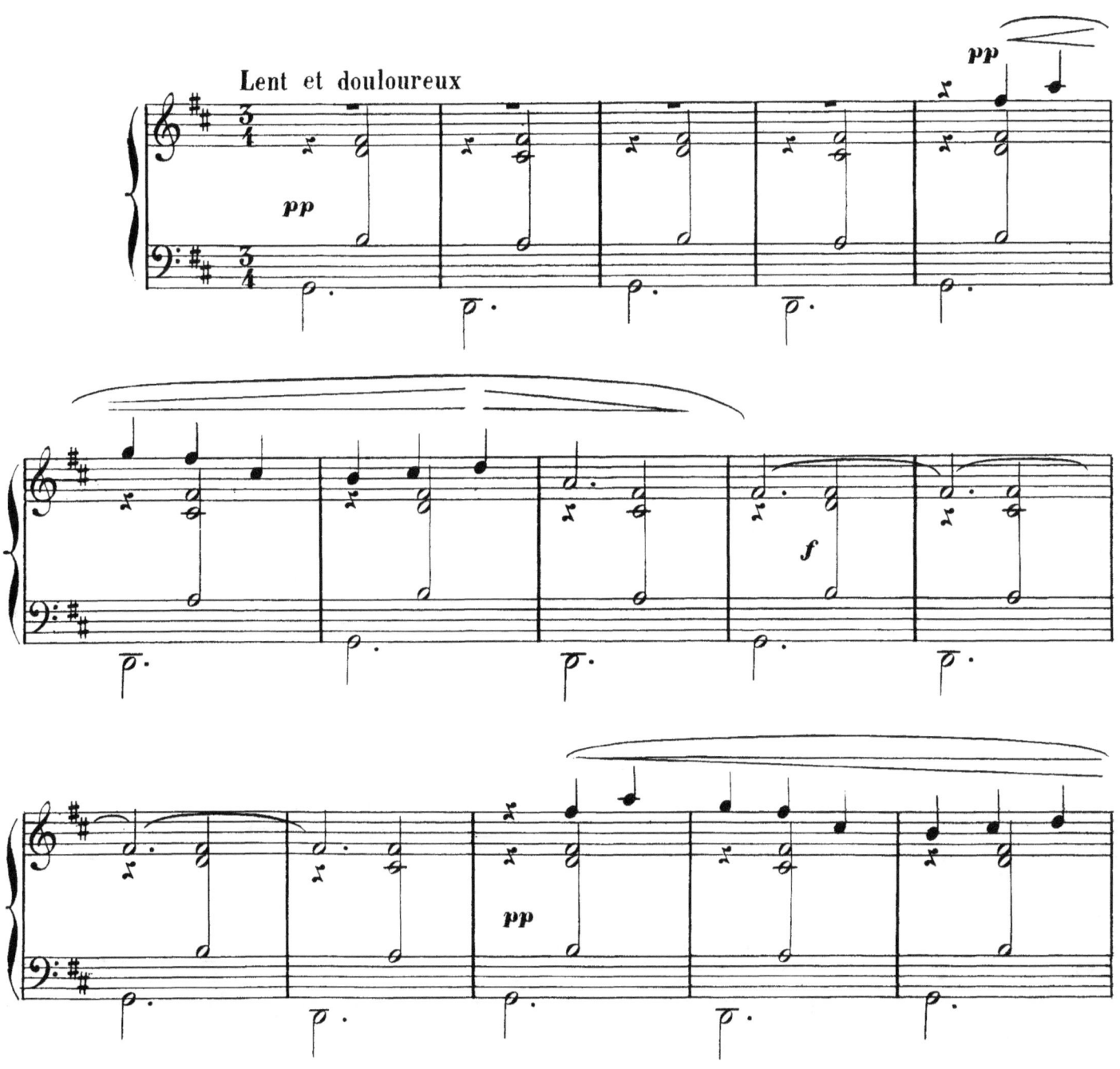

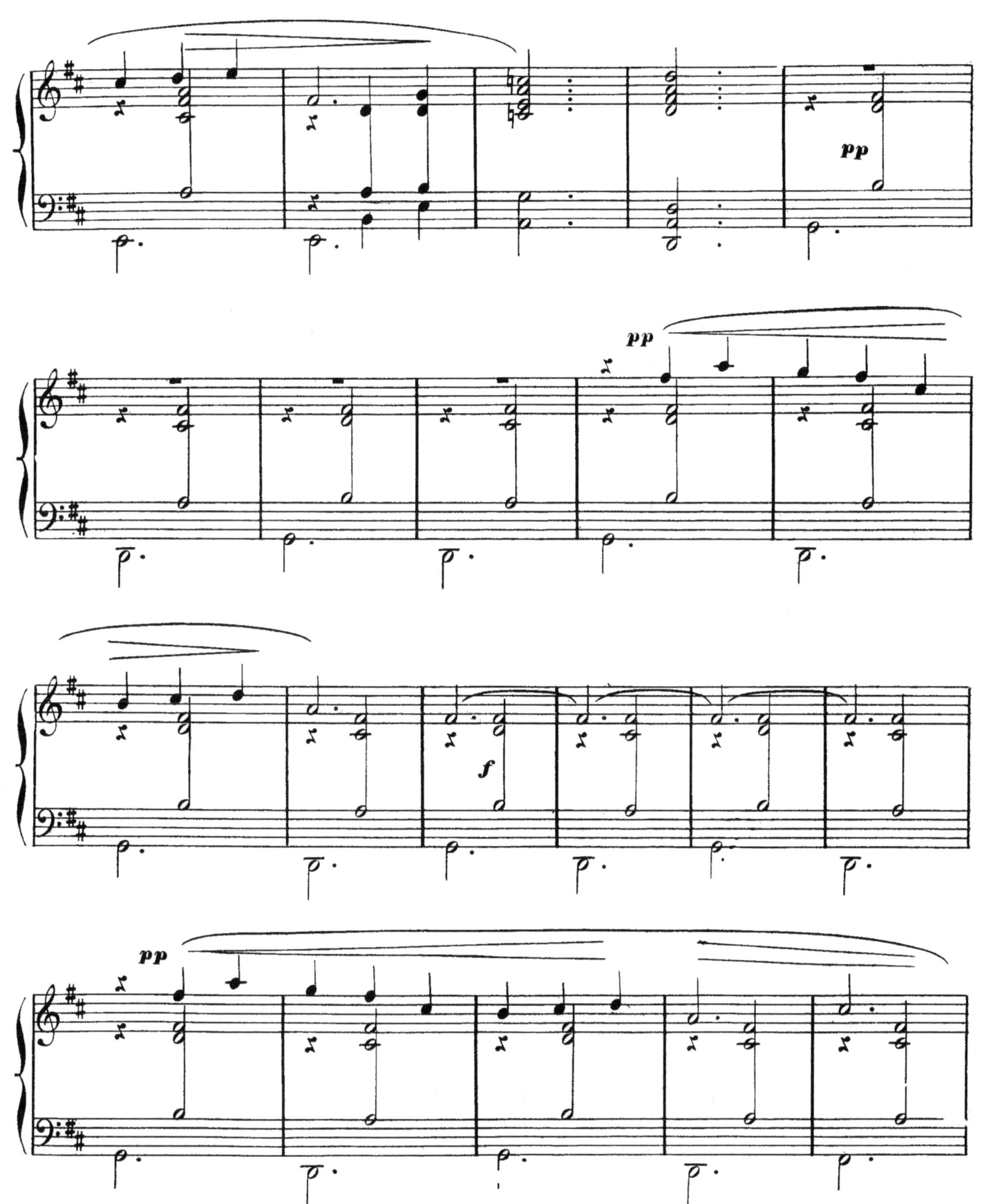

à CONRAD SATIE

2.ᵉᵐᵉ GYMNOPÉDIE

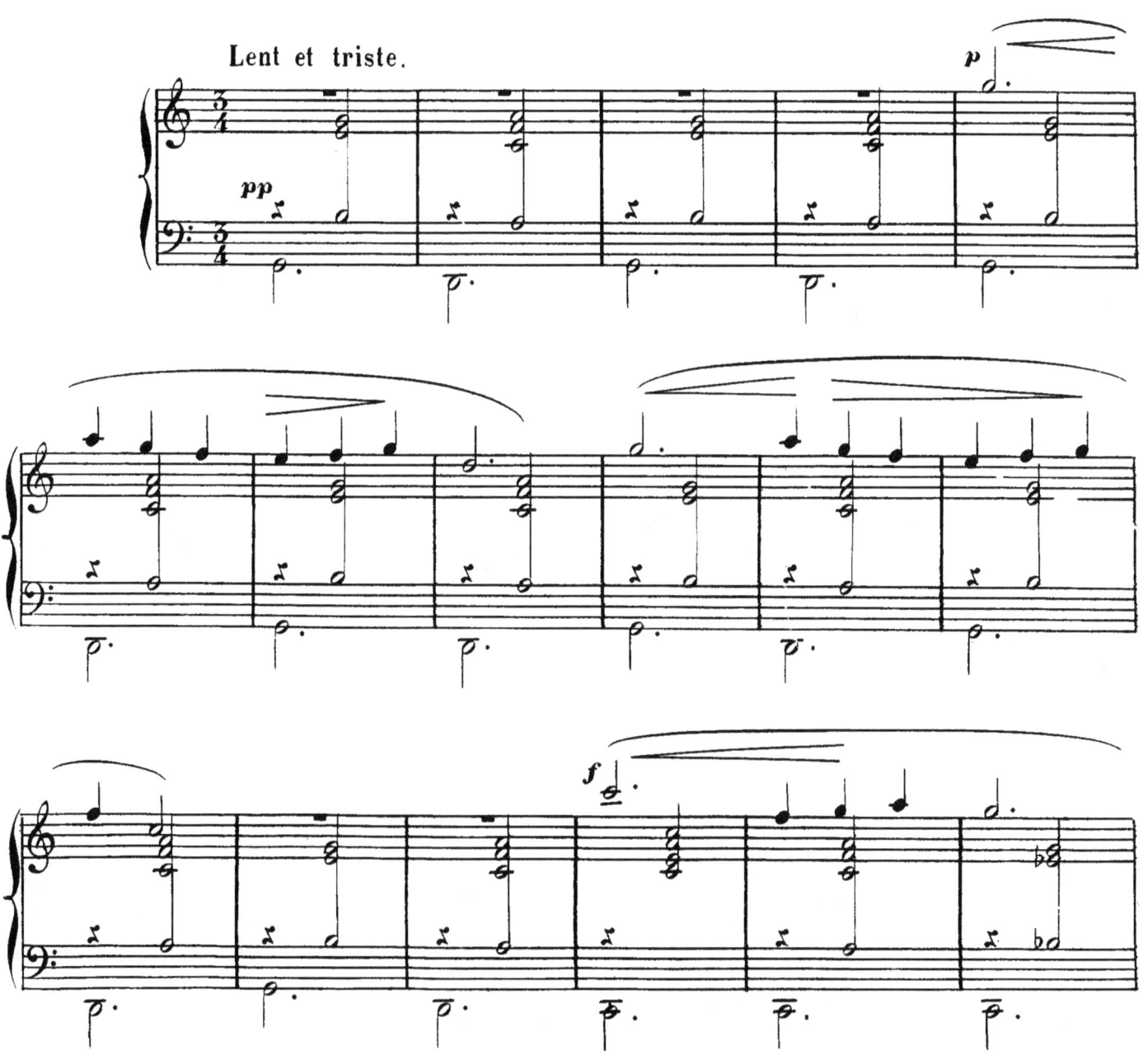

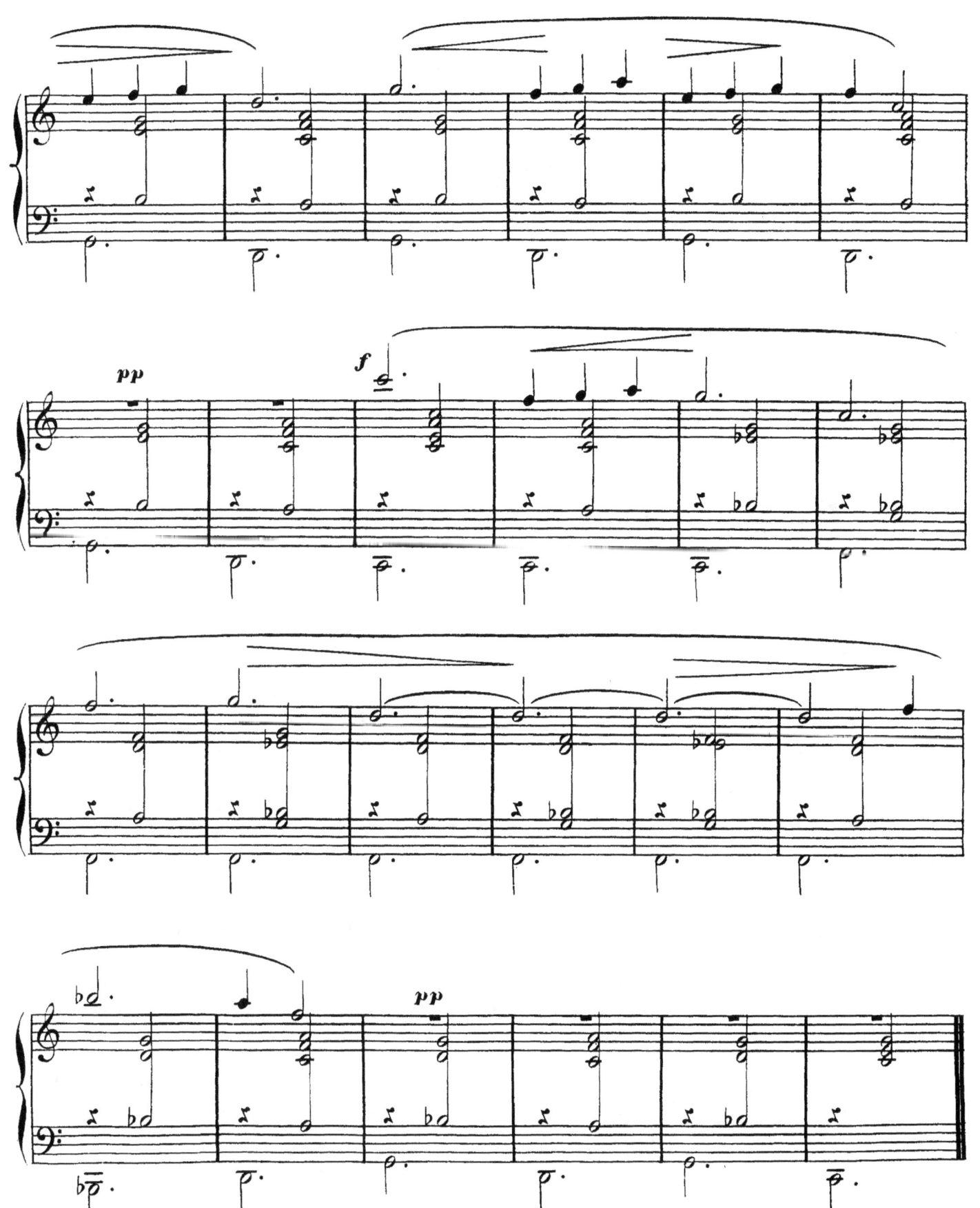

A CHARLES LEVADÉ

3.ᵐᵉ GYMNOPÉDIE

www.ingramcontent.com/pod-product-compliance
Lightning Source LLC
LaVergne TN
LVHW080934021225
826854LV00015B/970